LET'S PLAY SPORTS!

BASKETBALL

by Tessa Kenan

TABLE OF CONTENTS

WORDS TO KNOW

court

dribbles

hoop

net

passes

shoots

LET'S PLAY!

Let's play basketball!

This is a basketball court.

There is a hoop on each end.

basketball

This player dribbles the ball.

She passes the ball.

He shoots!

It goes in the net.

They score two points!

Do you want to play?

LET'S REVIEW!

What is this basketball player doing?

INDEX